The Stories of A Lost Soul

M. L. Searcy

Presentation by *BookLeaf Publishing*

Web: www.bookleafpub.com

E-mail: info@bookleafpub.com

ISBN: 978-93-95950-20-6

First edition 2022

DEDICATION

I'd like to dedicate this book to my grandma GG, Pamela Ebert, for always being my number one fan and being there for me through my rollercoaster no matter what. She has made me the strong woman that I am today. Without her nothing is possible.

ACKNOWLEDGEMENT

I'd like to thank Jace Walsh for encouraging me to challenge myself, and giving me the confidence to put my raw soul out in this cruel world.

PREFACE

This book is a tribute to all of me. I dig into my soul, and scrape out the rawest pieces for you. Read along and ride my rollercoaster of passion, love, life, loss, grief, and healing.

Your Name Here

I often catch myself saying my own name, only to find that it sounds strangely unfamiliar....

All of Me

I am a poet.
I find beauty in the darkest of things.

To you, they are just words.
Silly,
Little words.

But to me,
They are vital.

As essential as the air you breathe,
So ungratefully.

To experience my art,
my poetry,
my love,
Is to experience all in one.

You do not experience
one,
without the other.
That is why I love it.

I need it because
It sets something

a flame,
inside of me.

It is
my soul,
and subconscious,
standing naked in a crowd
with goosebumps covering her skin.

All of this,
with the power to be selfish
with it,
or to be
careless with it.

I love it, because it can be all of me,
or it can me none of me.

Lullaby

Your voice is my sweet lullaby.
and my breathtaking sunrise.
Eyes open and I see two green skies.
They bid me good morning.
They bid me goodnight.

Oh sweet lullaby,
With intense times
and sorrowful goodbyes, I cry.
You are there to wipe my flustered
cheeks dry.

Oh sweet lullaby,
your touch is my safety blanket and my sweet,
sweet peace of mind.
Lips touch and I take it.
They bid me again good morning.
They bid me again good night.

Love Is A Hate Crime

Who new?
That somebody
Could effect my body

With such an intensity,
That the universe
Could send butterflies
Through the core of my soul

And also a hate
So intense,
It feels like acid
Coursing through my veins.

Good Girl

Good Girl
Don't feel.

Take this!
Just heal.

Worry later!
Sit still.

While your broken bones
Steal

What you worked so hard to reveal.
"You're lucky you weren't killed!"

"It's a miracle!"
"God's will"

If I could, I'd strike a deal
For my precious time back.

That fate had the nerve
To steal.

Gravesite of My Mind

Dig into the gravesite of my mind
and find

Every little dirty secret
I left behind.

And every gesture,
that made me feel kind.

Find the memories.
And when I sip wine,
At the end of the night

Just know
It is to pass time.

To find,
The reason

I stay kind.
Even when I'm broken and blind.

Thirsty

I don't want to be your Sun and Stars
I want to be your Moon
Pulling you in, like the tides.

Kiss every inch of the surface of your sea.
So that you may taste the salt on my lips,
and grow thirsty for more
of me...

Scotch

Scotch warms my belly like your love in a
midnight storm;

and your giggle sounds like sunshine
So radiant, that it beamed through

and shattered my eardrums.

Your Eyes

Your eyes,
Beg for,
My body,
Craves for,
Your soul

Your eyes,
Make the mid day skies,
Look mischievous.

Like they gossip,
Throughout the night
And tell each other lies.

Fragile, Handle with Care

Your touch soothes every nerve in my body.
And it leaves me,
Craving for more.

It leaves me reminiscing,
about it,
for hours.

As if I could still feel
Your hands,
In the small,
Of my back.

And your lips
On mine,
So softly.

Like a kiss
On a babies cheek.
Scared, that the slightest touch
Could cause harm.

Like handling,
A precious
Gem.

Selfish

The way your hands feel on my skin is a whole
new feeling,
one I've never felt before.

An ecstasy of sorts,
the intimacy of your skin on mine is a high
in and of itself.

It is freshly shaved legs
on silky smooth clean sheet.

It is a crisp tart wine on the back of your throat
on a busy Friday night.

It is all the things I long for but am too selfless
to enjoy.

You make me selfish.

Hometown Horror

Mountain's mirrored over glass.
The same place men fish for bass.

The same place
We'd go when we would skip class
Where we drank underage and got sand in our
ass.
Memories to last.

Hills dry these days,
All weeds no grass.

A place where tourists used to flock in masses.
Now the gravesite for our ancestors ashes.

Tequila Smiles

I got drunk that night.
Not to celebrate,
But to mask
my disappointment...
In tequila smiles.

-On My Engagement Day

Take A Long Ride

Can I just disappear?
Is it possible?
If I just close my eyes and click my heals
together.
1
2
3
Or maybe?
The ruby slipper's is what I need?

All jokes aside I'd rather die...
Or take a long ride.

Somewhere we can hide
and love wholeheartedly.
Kiss under the moon
and see a raven without starling.

No more fear of feelings
No more tears,
for the broken heart in me.

Forgive & Forget

Forgive We Cannot Forget We Will Never

Because forgotten is a thought
we think of never.

Because we believe in your pride.
We will,
stay by your side

Until the end of time.

And as death as your bride,
We'll always cry.

Until the end of time,
we'll side,
with you
'til the end of the nether.

For in spirit we are together.

As justice still tethers,
forgive we will never.

-Thoughts On My Brother's Murder

Embrace Me

Embrace my soul
with yours.
Let them embrace each others pain.

Putting a perimeter around it,
So it cannot grow
and giving it a pathway to leave.

An open gateway.
An acceptance of itself,
So strong
That it can be free,
A relief.

Getting Better

Is it depression that causes obsession?
An escape for my lost affection?

With no confession, you hold it in your heart for
pure protection.
From you and all of your lost affections.

The counselor says,"The fact that you didn't turn
back means you're getting better."

But i've pretended like it's night forever.
Sometimes I still flinch, from a simple pinch.

Token

My eyes are sunken by the rivers of this battle.
I tell myself take it as a token,
of your life that is unspoken.

Be ecstatic for another chance to be romantic.
Smell the roses, feel the beach air on your skin,
and you can't wait to feel the sand again.

I tell myself
I can't handle
what life
has thrown at me.
My battles.

Then I am reminded,
of words once spoken to me.

"You are broken, but your mind is as strong as
The Great Wall of China."

And I take that as a token of my life that is
unspoken.
I am ecstatic for my second chance at romance.

The Thief

There is a beast that walks among my mind.
He lives there rent free.

Takes my tears to fuel his demons.
Steals my dreams to place with screams.

Confiscates all of my cherished memories
and tortures me with court dates, testimonies too
gruesome for my mental health to handle.

Leaves me to commute to justify my brothers
murder.
To stand when he cannot.

He lives there sipping whisky i'm sure.
Enjoying his time, stuck in my mind.

Replacing the lively image of my brother, I keep
on repeat in my mind…
With pictures,
agonizing,
undeserving
plea deals
and evidence too gruesome for your thoughts to
subside.

They will tattoo themselves in my mind.
They'll stay scarred there until my end time.
Smiles and laughter are just here to hide,
the empty whole Angel left behind.

-On My Brother's Murder

Super Nova

Too many stars in the sky.
Too many bodies that lye.
In the Earth as it dries.

Too many pills we can buy,
To get ourselves high.

To mask all our feelings,
Just to get by.

Another day that goes by,
That we try to not want to die.

That we smile in person,
But shut the door to cry.

Too many stars in the sky,
To let this super nova die.

Blank Pages

23

Blank pages
remind me of all the
lost time
I spent,

waiting for the tides
to turn fine sand,
into precious pearls.